How to Write

a

Romance Novel

JUDY ANGELO

DEDICATION

***This book is dedicated to
aspiring and experienced writers alike***

Sometimes we need a kindly kick to get us going
(again)

CONTENTS

NOTE TO MY READERS

This is not your typical guide on writing romance. Instead of the usual focus on standard writing techniques (setting, dialogue, point of view, etc.), the goal of this guide is to provide you with the tools for presenting the kind of story that creates a compelling connection with your reader. Through creative use of the following techniques, you will claim her attention, captivate her curiosity, and keep her coming back for more.

INTRODUCTION

Are you serious about writing?

My Journey

I began my writing journey with the first in my **Bad Boy Billionaires** series, **Tamed by the Billionaire**. I had always loved feisty females and, in this story, I was determined to write about a heroine who was just that – feisty and fearless and full of spunk. Of course, in the end she would be tempered by the ultimate alpha male, the kind of man I would want to fall in love with, myself.

And, thus, was born **Tamed by the Billionaire**, the story of a spoiled rich girl who, according to a plan orchestrated by her own father, was made to work for a man determined to make her the kind of woman her father had always wanted his daughter to be. But who said the job would be easy? The hero certainly met his match when he found himself boss to a girl who was anything but a meek maiden. No, she was more like a vicious vixen. These were the kinds of characters who intrigued me and, so, I began to write these kinds of stories, stories that I loved.

From there, I went on to write **Maid in the U.S.A.,** a story with a very different heroine, a more reserved one, to be sure, but one who was still able to teach the billionaire bachelor a lesson on love.

Why do I mention these stories? I mention them to let you see that what made me get started was the fact that I was creating characters with whom I had fallen in love. In fact, if falling in love with several men at the same time is a sin, I'm guilty. I'm guilty of falling in love with every bold bachelor I have ever created.

So, what was step one in my journey? Falling in love with romance novels was the first step for me. That's the best place to get going - getting started in writing on a subject that sweeps you away. If you love romance, then write romance. Write a romance novel that you, yourself, will fall in love with. Write characters you can't resist. That's the key to connecting with readers, a critical component in writing. If you can connect, and your readers can love your characters the way you do, then you have a firm formula for success.

After having written over 50 novels (some published and some not yet published), I've learned a lot about writing romance novels, and I'm happy to share my key learnings with you. Now, let's get started.

But before we begin

Before we get into the meat of the matter, I have some words of advice. First, know your genre. You already know you love to read romance novels. But what kind of romance novel do you like to read? What kind of romance novel would you like to write? Are you a fan of contemporary romance, paranormal romance, or young adult? Decide on the kind of story you would like to write, the one you're most comfortable with, and then do your research.

What do I mean? There's nothing that beats reading romance novels in the genre in which you plan to market your books. Read voraciously. Get to know the language of your selected genre. Get to know the characters. Do these readers love alpha males, or a calm and serious soul? Do the readers like a spicy story with sizzling sex or are they simply looking for a riveting romance which keeps the bedroom door closed?

Next, check the best-seller lists. See what sells. It makes no sense for you to get started on this journey, dedicating your precious time to writing several stories, when there is no market for it. Now, if you're writing, simply for the pleasure of writing, then maybe that will work for you. Somehow, though, I think you'll want to make some money from all your effort.

Another word of advice, if you don't already know this - decide/determine if you are a pantser or a plotter. As a pantser, you will 'write by the seat of your pants', not knowing where the story is going, but just letting it take you along for the ride. If you are a plotter, you will sit down and write an outline, planning your story from beginning to middle to end, knowing exactly where you will be going in every chapter, right to the end.

That is exactly my style - I am a plotter. An unapologetic plotter. I will not begin my story until I know how it starts, what happens in the middle, and how it wraps up at the end. I'm always so afraid of sitting down, writing without a plan, and then writing myself into a corner from which I cannot escape.

I know each person is different but, based on my personal experience with multiple stories, my advice is to use the technique of the plotter - preparing an outline before you even begin to write your story. I have found that, with a detailed outline, I can determine ahead of time if there are any holes in my story. As I said, each individual is different, and you must know what works best for you. However, I cannot help you with the pantser's technique. I can show you what has worked for me and has helped me hit the top 100 in Amazon's Contemporary Romance Best-Seller List multiple times. It has helped me captivate my readers and connect with them in a way that has kept them reading, right to the end. How do I know that? They told me in their e-mails and reviews.

So, in a nutshell, decide on your romance genre, read voraciously in that category, take note of what works - characters, pacing, voice, etc. - and decide on how you will execute - will you be a pantser, working your way through the story as the ideas come to you, or will you be a plotter, preparing your outline from the outset, knowing exactly how your story starts and how it will end? Once you've decided on all of this, you're ready to roll.

So, let's go...

CHAPTER ONE

YOUR COVER

The number one thing that you can use to capture the attention of your reader is your cover. You may have the sweetest story in the world but if your cover does not speak to that story, then you've lost the battle before it's even started.

Have you ever heard the saying, 'a picture is worth a thousand words'? Well, that definitely applies to stories. If your book has a captivating cover then, at the least, your reader will be more likely to click on that link. She will be so intrigued that she will want to know what lies behind that cover. Now, if you achieve that, to get her to go in and check out your book, you've taken step one on that journey to becoming a best-selling author.

So, what's so special about the cover? What should it do for the potential reader? The reader should see images that provide a promise. This should be a promise that she will be satisfied with a sensational story. That is not to say that there aren't successful romance novels which may not have the most captivating cover. In fact, there may be super successful novels which have covers featuring nothing but still photos (scenery, flowers, a red apple, etc.).

But you want to make this as easy as possible, don't you? And what appeals to the market right now? Characters on the cover, characters to whom your reader can relate. And now, with the high level of competition, it is even more important to have a professionally made cover, one that does not scream amateur. The good thing is, there are so many artists available online, you are bound to find a talented one at a good price. Just search. You can start with websites such as Fiverr.com and Upwork.com.

For imagery, try to find characters who captivate. Don't know where to start looking? Try iStockphoto.com or Bigstockphoto.com, or others like these. They have reasonably priced photos. You just have to search (do a Google search for stock photos). The key, though, is to place those images in the hands of a cover designer with a good eye, one who will take a simple photograph and make it a masterpiece.

Another thing to note when doing your cover is to select images that are appropriate to your genre. Writing a sweet romance? Forget about those men with their shirts off, chests bare. That sends one message, maybe not the message you're trying to send. Be sure to take note of the covers in your selected genre. So, if you've chosen to write a sweet romance, select images that suit – a demure damsel or a more mature macho man. If hot and steamy, then go for it with the bare chests. But don't mix the two. Don't confuse your reader. That's when you put yourself at risk of getting negative reviews.

In fact, before you begin working on your cover, why not check out the covers of books that have been successful so far? Go ahead. Visit the Amazon, Apple or Kobo romance best-seller lists and see what covers are popular in your genre, and what covers sell. Check Scribd, Barnes and Noble and Google Play, among others. See if you can match them in design and quality. Quality does not necessarily mean a high price. You just want something that matches up to what you see in the store (in terms of quality of the image).

CHAPTER TWO

YOUR TITLE

The second important thing you can do to attract the attention of your potential reader is to hook her with a title that promises reading pleasure. By pleasure, I don't necessarily mean something sweet, like a gentle romance. What I mean is something that intrigues, something that piques her curiosity. It gets her going, gets those reading taste buds tingling. It gets her wanting to grab hold of that story.

Many times, for me, it's the title that gets me started on writing a story. I may come up with a title which I absolutely love, and yet I have absolutely no idea what the story is about. However, by the time I think on the title for a while, I've come up with a story to match. Take, for example, Her Indecent Proposal. Did I even know what the story was going to be about? No. But I thought of the title, it appealed to me, and I decided I was going to write a story to match. I mulled it over in my mind and, before you knew it, I was busy preparing the outline. I was writing a story to match my title.

But the key was, I had a tantalizing title. I had a title that was designed to inspire intrigue and make my reader really curious. What kind of proposal was it? And why the heck was it indecent?

And then, there are those titles which are a play on well-known words and familiar phrases. Here are a couple of my titles which fit the bill: **Rome for the Holidays**, **Beauty and the Beastly Billionaire.** Ever heard the phrase, 'Home for the holidays'? Do you know a story called Beauty & The Beast? These are phrases to which your reader can relate. These titles appeal to the reader's subconscious and, whether she knows it or not, she is inclined to approach the story in a more positive way.

So, at the risk of belaboring the point, let me say this: take your title seriously. Reel in your reader with a title that tantalizes, titillates, and takes her on that terrific trip with you.

CHAPTER THREE

YOUR BLURB

Next on the list of table-turning techniques is your blurb. That's the next thing your reader will take note of, in her exploration of what you have to offer. Don't take it lightly. It's the blurb that will pull her in, and actually get her to start reading your story. And that's what you want, isn't it? You want her to get a peep of the promise that lies within.

And so, what do you do?

You take your blurb seriously, considering it a very important part of your marketing plan. This is where you get the opportunity to provide the details of your story. But not just any detail. You will want to select the information that will intrigue your reader, hook her, and then leave her wanting more. This is where you will present a summary of your story, providing information that you know will capture the reader's interest, but not enough to provide any answers. Not at all. You want them to wonder. You want them to yearn for the answer to the question you posed in your blurb. Will these two ever end up together?

Here is where you introduce your main characters.

This is the place where you show why your hero and heroine are worth reading about. Is he a bad and bold bachelor, so audacious that he's too alluring to resist? Is she an adorable rebel, one whose charm will draw you in? Are they young and spirited or more mature but still made for major magic (in the bedroom, that is)?

Then, there's the next big question: is there conflict? What is the reason to read this story? After reading many romance novels (I certainly hope you have), I'm sure you recognize the importance of conflict and tension in a story. You should know, by now, that it's downright difficult to hold the attention of the reader if all is going sweetly and smoothly. Tension grabs the attention. Use it! (With conflicts thrown in along the way).

Your setting can also be presented in your blurb but be careful. Don't spend too much time on the setting when what the reader really wants to know is if these two characters will ever connect. Your goal is to make her curious, so, if you present setting in your blurb, make it work for you – use it actively, to support the intrigue of the story or to create an appropriate backdrop for your characters.

Quickly move on and present your characters in all their glory, good or bad. Make the reader want to know them better. The key to a successful story is the characters. That's who your reader wants to get to know and love. So, make that blurb work for you. Make the reader love your characters even before she's even met them.

Here's an example of a blurb that creates curiosity.

To Catch a Man (in Thirty Days or Less) - the **Bad Boy Billionaires** series, Book 8:

How Do You Catch A Man in Thirty Days?

Indiana Lane is in a pickle. She must find a man, fall in love and get married...all within the space of thirty days. How in the world can she pull this off? And then she runs into Stone Hudson - or, more accurately, he runs into her - and that's when the adventure begins.

Stone Hudson has met his match. He's used to having women fall all over him...and then he meets Indie, a woman who tells it like it is. And, worse, she dares tease him wherever and whenever she desires. Stone is intrigued, to say the least, but then his heart is snagged on a wire from which there is no escape.

Will the wedding bells ring for Indie, and will they ring in time? Thirty days is not a lot of time...

So, what was the purpose of this blurb? It was designed to get the reader past the cover, past the intrigue introduced in the title, and into the reading of a super-tempting tale. This is where there is the elaboration of the intrigue that was introduced in the title. This is also where the main characters are introduced in the most intriguing way, with that question with the capital Q – will these two characters (who I already love) ever be together? In a word, this is the hook – the way you reel the reader in and get her to take that all-important action, the act of clicking on the BUY button.

Never underestimate the power of your blurb. Make it a PROMISE OF PLEASURE that your reader will not be able to resist.

CHAPTER FOUR

JUDY ANGELO'S LAW OF FIRSTS

I'm a fan of strong first impressions. Because of this, I pay attention to the first impression each of my fiction works gives. In the case of stories, I am careful with specific things...my first line, my first paragraph, my first scene, and my first chapter. These are what provide my readers with their first impression of the story. It may make or break the story. It may make the reader decide to jump in and give it a try or just pass it by. And so, I'll share my Law of Firsts with you.

The important first sentence

The first sentence of your story is all important. As I said, it creates the first impression that your reader will get, of your story. More than that, it is the hook that will make her actually begin to read. Do you want to start your story with a description of some mundane thing? Do you really want to spend precious time, your time and your reader's, in setting the stage with a detailed description of scenery? This is the twenty-first century - the age of haste. Who has the time for all that? So, now that you've actually begun writing your story, get your next tool to work for you. This is your second hook after the blurb (or the fourth, if you also count the cover and the title). The very first sentence in your story should get your reader to say, "Oh, my goodness! What's going on here?" This first sentence should make her want to enter your world to find out what is happening. It is therefore all important.

After a few tries, and a few stories under my belt, I found out how important it was. In my earlier books, I tried it without knowing what I was doing. Luckily, it worked. In later books, I tried a slower start, and got a slower build. That was when I realized how effective an opening sentence really was. I recommend that, as you embark on your writer's journey, you think of starting your story with a scintillating sentence, an opening that will intrigue your reader enough to make her want to enter your world.

Here are some examples for you:

Tamed by the Billionaire

Roman Steele stared across the boardroom table at his long-time business associate. "So, basically, you're telling me she's a spoiled brat."

Okay, so I cheated. Those were the first two sentences, not just one. Forgive me. It was my very first story in the **Bad Boy Billionaires** series. I was just learning. But still, do you see how I started the story? I started with a note of intrigue. The reader is now put in the frame of mind to want to know more. Who is this person they're talking about? Why is she considered a brat? What has she done? What will happen next? So, from the start of the story, the reader is hooked. That reader will want to know more. That's the role of your first sentence.

Here's another example:

Daddy by December

"I want her."

Before we even get into the story, we know that something's going to happen. I want her? Why? Who is she? And who are you, to want somebody, and to say it so boldly and so blatantly? What does it mean? Do you have the power to possess someone, to demand the person's presence? It sounds like you think you can control her. Do you see what has happened here? The reader's curiosity has been sparked. This was achieved from the first line. The mystery is now making the reader muse, his mind making him move even further into the story. It's a mystery that will not be solved unless he continues reading. Hence, the power of the first line.

And here's a third example –

Bedding her Billionaire Boss

With a name like Rockford Saint Stephens, I can just imagine what he's like. Probably a pompous ass.

What does this say about the story? It immediately says there will be conflict, and who loves conflict more than a romance reader? And we haven't even started the story yet. Regardless, we've hooked the reader and now all we have to do is build on that mystery, keep reeling our fish in until it's right there in our basket. I won't give you any more examples. I think I've made my point.

The first line or first sentence of your story is all powerful. Do not underestimate it. Value it. Make it work for you.

Now we go to:

The (Even More Important) First Paragraph

We've hooked them with our first line, but the job is not yet done. Now is where we have to reel them in. First paragraphs are primarily important because they heighten the intrigue and give the reader a reason to read on. This is where you yank on the hook even harder. You jerk the line back and make sure it sinks in - all the way.

Here's what I mean:

Billionaire's Blackmail Bride

Sweet. The gods must be smiling down on him today. Lani Donatelli was sitting right here in his office and she was in big trouble. Could things get any better?

That's it, guys. Nothing but a few lines, but what we have done with this paragraph is, we have set the stage for a story that promises pure pleasure, if you can call it that. If not, at minimum, it promises some kind of conflict. And that's what romance novels are all about, isn't it? Conflict which finally resolves in a satisfying story of romance.

When it comes to your first paragraph, need I say anything more? You've hooked them with the first line, but that was just an initial insertion of that hook. Now you've got to make it sink in. And do it swiftly - in the first paragraph. Want another example?

The Billionaire Next Door

"Oh hell, no."

The words exploded from Solie's lips as she stared out the kitchen window. Ever since that flippin' man moved in next door, he'd been nothing but trouble. First, his stupid robotic lawnmower smashed up her hedge when he'd been landscaping. Then, his great dane wouldn't stop howling in the middle of the night. And now this. A friggin' construction crew in the backyard?

Okay, so maybe that wasn't the most elegant example, but you get my point. The first paragraph was effective in establishing a world in which there was opportunity for conflict. It was a promise. It was designed to hook the reader, sink that hook in, and begin the process of reeling him in. And, if you're a reader who loves conflict, you're going to read this story.

In a project I did with a fellow writer, Melody Anne – a Kindle Worlds contribution - I presented my first erotic short story, **The**

Billionaire's Bold Bet.   Here's how it started:

"I can have any woman I want. There isn't even a question about that".   Dante Perakis leaned back in his chair and clasped his hands behind his head, a satisfied smile on his lips.

Now, if that isn't an invitation to read on, I don't know what it is.

So, what can I say about first paragraphs? First paragraphs are critical to the success of your story. After you've hooked the reader with the first line, then you go and sink the hook in - deep - with the first paragraph. You don't want that hook to slip out. You want her coming closer and closer to your boat until you can grab her and haul her all

the way in, right beside you in the boat.

And so, with that done, we can now look to the next stage in the adventure: the first scene.

The (Still More Important) First Scene

So, the first paragraph got him into the boat. But don't be fooled. Your work is still far from done. You don't want him in the boat, flopping and flailing, fighting to get out. No. By this time, you want him so captivated with your creation (your story, of course) that he can do nothing but acquiesce.

It is the job of the first scene to make him do that. While he is resting there, caught by the first paragraph, struggling to catch his breath, this is when you ramp things up. At this point, while he is in his weakened state, under no circumstance do you ease the tension. No way. On the contrary, this is when you move in for the kill (sorry for the vocal violence, but it has to be done). While still trapped in the promise made by your first paragraph, you finish him off in the intensified intrigued introduced in your first scene (which, if you're doing it right, will be scintillating).

Now, let's have a look at one of my earlier stories:

To Catch a Man (in Thirty Days or Less)

"Are you kidding me?"

Randolph Marshall shook his head. "I'm dead serious. You have until October twenty-three or you forfeit fourteen million dollars."

"Fourteen million…" Indiana Lane's voice trailed off as she stared across the desk at the attorney. "No, you've got to be kidding me." She looked around the room. "I'm on 'Candid Camera', right? Or one of those other crazy prank shows?" She began to chuckle as she turned to look back at him.

"Miss Lane, trust me. I do not have time for pranks." Exasperation dripped from each word. "I'm an old man with a bad heart. I don't play games. I tell it as it is. Do you understand me?"

Indie's smile began to fade as she stared back at the now frowning man. Okay, so he really was serious. He was shaking his graying head and looking at her like he wanted to give her a sharp rap on the knuckles. Ouch.

"Yes," she said, gripping the arms of the chair, "I understand you but...but he hardly even knew me."

Marshall looked unimpressed. "He seems to have known you well enough to want to make you a rich woman. Under certain conditions, of course."

"But...but..." She was spluttering again. Come on, Indie, this is so not like you. You've negotiated with guerilla fighters and warlords and you're *thrown upside down by this? She drew in a slow, deep breath then got up and shoved her hands deep into her trouser pockets. Her brain worked better when she was standing.*

"So, let me get this straight. Based on the stipulations in my uncle's will, I have to find a man in the next..." she frowned, thinking, "...thirty days, fall in love, and get married in order to inherit this fourteen million dollars?"

Randolph cocked a grizzly eyebrow. "Nobody said anything about falling in love."

"Well, I can't very well just run off and marry the next man I run into, can I? One would hope I'd at least feel something for him...and he, for me." She stopped talking when she saw the attorney's expression. Was the man laughing at her?

"A real idealist, I see." His smile was broader than the Cheshire Cat's.

That got her riled up. "And who says I want his

money, anyway?" The man was looking too smug and it was pissing her off. Big time. "Money has never been the biggest thing in my life, Mr. Randolph Marshall. And neither has marriage. I can do without both of them-"

"Yes, Miss 'Save-The-World'. I know. And that's exactly why your uncle did what he did. Don't you worry. He filled me in on all the details."

Now, on top of pissing her off. he was confusing the heck out of her. "What details?"

"Remember that conversation you had with him right after your mother's funeral?"

She frowned. "That was nine years ago."

"Yes," Randolph said with a nod. "You were twenty-one years old and you sat in the library spouting off your idealistic philosophies to Samuel, about not wanting to get married or have children. There are too many homeless kids in the world for you to even think of starting a family of your own.

Isn't that what you said?"

Indie straightened to her full five-foot seven inch height and frowned at Marshall. What was he getting at? "Yeah, so what? I still think the same way."

Marshall nodded slowly. "Ah-ha. And that's what your uncle was afraid of." He leaned forward and propped his elbows on the desk. "You're going to be thirty years old in thirty days, Indiana. Thirty. Think of it. That old, and no man and no kids. No life, except for running off to the favelas of Brazil to save orphans. or chopping through the bushes and jungles of Colombia to search out drug dealers selling girls as sex slaves. Where were you this time? Africa?"

"Haiti," she said, her tone sullen.

The lawyer heaved a sigh. "Haiti. And where next? Cambodia?" He shook his head. "Listen. Your uncle wants his bloodline to continue. He never had kids and you, his sister's child, are his only hope of that. He wanted you to get cracking while your eggs are still viable."

"He what?" Indie almost burst out laughing. The audacity of the man. "He actually said that?"

"Yes, and more, but..." Marshall put his hand up, "you don't want to know." He leaned back in his chair and clasped his hands behind his head. "So, are you on board? Can I cross you off my list of things to do this month, and consider this sealed and set?"

Indie could only shake her head in disbelief. Between the lawyer and her now dead uncle, she didn't know which one was battier. They'd probably both been smoking the same...prohibited substance.

"Now you listen to me, Mr. Marshall." She fixed him with a glare of defiance. "I have two things to say to you. Number one, I don't want a

single dime of Uncle Sam's fourteen million dollars. I've gotten along quite well without his help and will continue to survive, I'm sure. And number two," she raised an eyebrow, "if he'd wanted me to be married, barefoot and pregnant by age thirty he should have spoken a heck of a lot earlier than September twenty-three."

For a long moment Marshall just stared at her, his lips pursed, then he nodded solemnly. "Well said, but let me implore you to think about it. You're so concerned about doing good in the world, do you know how much more you could do with fourteen million dollars?" He paused as if to let that sink in. "And as for the timing, I think I know what happened." He glanced down, shifted a couple of papers, then picked up the will. He reached for his glasses, put them on, then peered at the document. "Yes," he said with a sigh, "I was right. He miscalculated your age. When he updated this four years ago, he had you down as twenty-four years old but you were actually twenty-

five." He looked up at her, peering over the top of his glasses like an old owl. "I guess he was planning to tell you but was biding his time, watching to see if things would work out. Probably thought he had at least a few more months before he had to tackle you on such a touchy subject." He shrugged. "Who was to know he'd have been taken out by a heart attack at age sixty-six?"

Marshall's speech had Indie staring at him in shock. She was so worked up, she didn't know what to say. Then, she snorted. "Yeah, right. He thought I was a year younger? Do you realize, if he hadn't died when he did, I would have soon passed his stupid deadline for me? I'll be thirty in a month."

"Yeah, well." Marshall shrugged. "If he'd lived, he probably would have updated the will. The pity is, he never got a chance to realize or correct his miscalculation. And, with him being dead, you're stuck with it."

"This is so stupid," Indie muttered, as she began to pace the room. "Stupid, stupid."

"I know. But it is what it is. Fourteen million dollars or zilch. Your call." The lawyer began to slide the documents back into the case. "You know where to find me, Indiana. I leave everything in your hands. Just remember the date – October twenty-three, by midnight."

And with that, Indie knew she was being dismissed. The man had other clients to deal with; other, more pressing business. He was probably checking the clock to make sure she didn't run over her portion of his 'billable hour', or whatever it was lawyers called it.

And, at the same time he was dismissing her, he'd thrown her normally well-ordered life into a whirlpool of indecision. Where in the world should she go from here? And if she did decide to fulfill Sam's condition, where the heck should she start looking for a man to marry...in thirty days?

******

What did we achieve with this opening scene? First, we caught the attention of the reader and made her start the story. Second, we established a dilemma designed to drive her to distraction (well, we hope so). Third, we left her with a need for knowledge. It's a mystery in the making, a serious situation which must be resolved. But how? That's what the reader needs to know. And that's what will eat away at her until she is rewarded with an answer.

Now, let's try another:

Beauty and the Beastly Billionaire

"Excuse me?"

"I said, come here." The man's voice was like granite, his dark eyes drilling into her, his stance rigid. And he'd said the words like she must not

keep him waiting.

Ellie tilted her chin upward, determined not to show any hint of fear. She would stand up to this brute of a man even though he might be a good foot taller than she was. She would not be intimidated by anyone, regardless of who he was.

The man folded his arms across his chest and glared at her but he did not say another word. It was as if he thought that was enough to make her move.

She didn't budge.

"Do you want this job or not?" His tone was as harsh as the arctic. "Come over here so I can look at you." He jerked his head toward the huge bay window of the penthouse office suite. "In the natural light."

Ellie drew in her breath and then she tightened her lips. His question had done the trick. It was that word...job...that yanked her out of her mutiny and made her curl her fingers around her purse instead. The answer to his insolent question was yes, she wanted the job. She needed it. Desperately. And that was the only reason why she took one tentative step forward and then another...and another...until she was standing a mere three feet away from him.

The hardness in the man's glare gave way to a glint of triumph. "Closer." He said that one word and then he waited. He knew she would comply soon enough. It was so painfully obvious that he was the one in control.

Ellie cleared her throat. "How much closer do you want me to come? Can't you see me well enough from there?"

"No. I want you right here." He bit the words out then stabbed at a spot just a foot away from where he stood, his face darkening with impatience. At that moment he looked like, if she didn't move, he would make her.

So she moved. Ellie took that step that put her right by the window, exactly in front of him and there she stood, waiting for his next move. It was unnerving, being so close to this big, obviously powerful man. She felt out of her depth, like she should turn tail and run, but the agency had sent her. She was on the job. She couldn't back out now.

He caught her off guard, making her gasp when his hand suddenly shot out to cup her chin. She tried to step back, to escape his touch, but he didn't let her. All she could do was stand there, a prisoner to this man, the touch of his hand branding itself into her skin.

Seeming satisfied that he had her exactly where he wanted her, he turned her face toward the sunlight that streamed in through the window. His gray eyes intense and unreadable, he regarded her for mere seconds and then he let her go. "You'll do," he said and he was turning away before the words were even out of his mouth.

And his words, so casual and so dismissive, stung. You'll do? Ellie knew she'd been selected to attend this meeting at the head office of Aura Cosmetics because she was considered one of the best that Lord Modeling Agency could offer. And all he could say was, you'll do?

"Be back here tomorrow at ten. The photo shoot will be long and it will be demanding. Make sure you get enough rest tonight. I don't want you getting tired and messing up the shoot." The man was already back in his seat, not even sparing her a glance as he swiveled to face his computer screen.

For a moment Ellie didn't know what to do. That was it? She'd been in this man's office all of three minutes. He'd examined her and then dismissed her. And she still didn't even know his name.

"Excuse me," she said for the second time that morning but this time she was frowning. She was normally a placid soul but the man's rudeness was

getting on her nerves. "Should I come here?" she asked. "To this office?"

He cut her a glance which clearly meant, *are you still here?* "Check in with the receptionist," he said, his voice brusque. "She will know where to send you."

"And whom should I ask for?" Two could play that game. Ellie could be just as cool, just as formal. She tilted her chin upward so she could look down her nose at him, literally. "We haven't been introduced."

That seemed to get his attention. The man's brows shot up and then they fell in a frown. "You don't know who I am?"

"No, I don't," she said in her best imitation of Queen Elizabeth II. Back at home in the Cayman Islands her friends at school always got a kick out of her play at royalty. It probably wouldn't have the same effect here but she would use it just the same.

The man pushed back in his chair and propped his elbows on the arms of his chair. "Who sent you up here?"

Glad she was finally commanding his full attention, Ellie lowered her chin and stared directly into his piercing eyes. "The agency told me I should meet with Jack Usher but as soon as we'd met he had his assistant deposit me here. Neither of them told me who you are."

"Hmm. Some creative director..." He'd grumbled under his breath but Ellie heard him. Obviously, he was not pleased. He looked up at her from where he sat by his desk and, as quickly as he'd moved earlier, he was up and striding to the window and back toward her. His movement, so lithe and determined, portrayed the latent power of a black panther, fearsome and fearless, ready to pounce on its prey.

He stuck his hand out, that same big, strong hand that had clasped her chin. "I am Amadeo

Castillo," he said, "owner of Cosmeticos Aurora. I'm sorry my creative director was rude and did not tell you this."

His creative director was rude? Ellie almost laughed. And what about him? This man, Amadeo Castillo, hadn't been an example of gentility, either. He was still holding his hand out so there was nothing for Ellie to do but take it. The minute she did he wrapped his fingers around her hand, enveloping it in his grip, holding it like he owned that part of her person. Or owned her...

And, for some strange reason, her heart began to race. It was a simple act, taking her hand, but it was like, in doing so, he now had possession of more than just her hand. He had possession of her. And she didn't like it.

"And I am Ellie Goldwell," she said, struggling to keep her voice calm and just a little bit frosty. And she was not going to say she was pleased to meet him. He might be the owner of this billion-dollar company but she was not impressed, not if it made this man feel he was above being polite. She'd heard enough and now she was ready to go so she began to pull her hand from his grasp. At least, she tried. He did not let her go.

"Ellie Goldwell," he said and the way he said her name, each syllable rolling off his tongue, made her draw in a stealthy breath. If he'd been trying to sound like a modern-day Don Juan he was doing a heck of a job. "Lord Agency's top model. You will be the new face of Cosmeticos Aurora, Ellie Goldwell. I have spoken."

I have spoken? That called for a lifting of the eyebrows. She didn't even hide her surprised amusement.

"There is no need for that look, Miss Goldwell. This is a very important position. You will represent my company to the world. I have final say on who fills this significant role." It was after he'd made that declaration, his eyes filled with unmistakable *pride, that he released her hand. "Now you must go. I told you to get your rest. Tomorrow you must be fresh and ready to work."*

He was dismissing her again, but Ellie did not acquiesce and turn toward the door like he obviously expected. She stayed right where she was and returned her hand to its previous position, clasping her purse in front of her like a shield. She tilted her head as she looked up at him. "I have a question," she said as he gazed down at her.

"A question." His brows lifted. "What question is that?"

"I was told to come to Aura Cosmetics of New York but you said your company is Cosmeticos Aurora. Twice. Are they one and the same?"

Amadeo Castillo smiled and for one brief moment he almost seemed human. It was a genuine smile, one that reached his eyes, those deep-gray eyes with thick, long lashes that would be the envy of any model. And his lips, so tight and firm just moments before, now curved in a way that made them seem so very kissable.

Ellie blinked. Where in the world was her mind taking her? She felt the heat of embarrassment begin to rise up her neck but she was rescued when the owner of the corporation began to speak.

"You have it right, Ellie Goldwell. They are one and the same." He nodded. "My company is based in Argentina and is called Cosmeticos Aurora. For my North American operation, though, it is called Aura Cosmetics. For the moment I am operating out of my New York office." And then, as quickly as his face had softened, it changed right back. "But now you must go," he said. "There is much I have to do today." And, just like that, he turned on his heel and headed toward his desk.

Taken aback by his abrupt departure, for a second Ellie did not move. Then, catching herself, she gave a quick shake of her head and turned toward the door. "Good day, Mr. Castillo." She threw the words, so cool and formal, over her shoulder as she went.

"The name is Amadeo," he said to her departing back. "That is what you must call me."

Ellie did not reply. As she opened the door and closed it firmly behind her she was frowning. What she must call him. Must. As if she had no choice in the matter. She had a feeling that what he'd just said would set the tone for what was to come.

Amadeo Castillo was a man who expected his 'subjects' to jump at his command. The question was, could she swallow her pride and play that humiliating role? She already knew this man would be a trial and a half. She could only pray that, before the job was done, she didn't lose her cool and put him in his place.

She would have a task of it, biting her tongue.

Heaven help her.

A promise of conflict, if there ever was one.

■■■

And there you go, folks. I think that's enough of the examples for now, but I think you get my drift.

Reel that reader in and dump her in the bottom of the boat, hook line and sinker.

The (Super Duper Important) First Chapter

So, we've got the fish out of the water and gasping in the bottom of the boat. Now it's time to get that sucker into the bucket. That's where your first chapter comes in. After she invests the time to read this whole first chapter, she's going to continue to the (hopefully fascinating) finish. It's highly unlikely that she'll get to the end of chapter one and then turn back - if you have the right hooks, that is.

This is where you must dedicate the time to flesh out the story, provide partial answers to some of the questions you posed with the first line, the first paragraph, and the first scene.

But don't reveal too much of your story, of course. You must maintain the mystery. What you are doing with your first chapter is establishing the main direction of your story, giving your reader an indication of what the story will be all about, but maintaining the intrigue. In my story, **Billionaire's Blackmail Bride**, from **The Castillos** series, the story begins like this:

Billionaire's Blackmail Bride

The opening of the story:

CHAPTER ONE

Sweet. The gods must be smiling down on him today. Lani Donatelli was sitting right here in his office and she was in big trouble. Could things go any better?

Leaning back in his chair, Ridge tented his fingers and regarded her through narrowed eyes. He was going to play tough even though he was laughing inside. She'd fallen right into his hands and he could not believe his luck.

"How's that again?" he asked, feigning confusion, watching the emotions flit across her face.

Lani gave an exasperated sigh. "Ridge Kent,

you heard every word I said. Why should I repeat myself?" The color rising in her cheeks, Lani was clenching and unclenching her hands like she was trying hard not to hop out of her chair, reach across the desk and strangle him. She looked so cute when she was angry, like a little pink pixie, so tiny she could pass for a kid as she sat there, lost in the big, black office chair. And it didn't help that she was sporting a super-short boy haircut. If he didn't already know her, he'd swear she was a stray twelve-year-old who'd wandered into his office.

But enough of admiring little Miss Cuteness. She'd asked a pointed question and he was only too willing to answer. "Maybe you should repeat yourself," he said, his tone cool, "because you really need this favor."

At his words Lani's eyes shot daggers and she looked like if she could have killed him with her glare she would have. "You don't need to rub it in," she said through clenched teeth.

"Oh, but I do," he replied. "I most certainly do."

And scene one ends this way:

"I'll give you the money," he said, his eyes never leaving hers, "on one condition."

Lani drew in a slow breath and her gaze grew even more suspicious. "What condition?"

"You can get your money to do your precious research project," he said, his tone even, "as long as you agree to marry me. I want you to be my wife for a year."

That declaration didn't get him the reaction he'd been expecting. Instead of the shock and horror he'd anticipated, Lani did the very opposite. The contrary girl burst out laughing.

"I heard you could be a joker, but this takes the cake. So, you're a businessman turned comedian now?" She wasn't shy with her guffaws. She was laughing so hard Ridge was thinking she might pitch forward and fall out of her chair.

But he wouldn't say a word. He would let her have her moment of fun and then he would set her straight. That grin would be wiped from her face soon enough.

When she finally calmed down enough to stop laughing and slide back in her chair Ridge got up and walked over to the credenza on top of which sat an ice bucket with bottles of water and juice. He glanced over at her. "Want one?" he asked.

She shook her head.

With a shrug he turned, grabbed a bottle of water and tipped it to his lips. He downed a third of it in one swig. As he lowered the bottle and replaced the cap, he regarded her with casual interest. "Ready to talk to me now?"

"About what?" she asked, a smile teasing the corner of her mouth. "Of course, you weren't serious."

He gave her a slow smile. "I'm dead serious."

It was only then that things seemed to sink in for Lani. The smile that had tickled her mouth disappeared. The lips that had just curled so prettily now turned thin and firm. "But why?" she asked, her tone half combative, half confused. "Why would you want me to marry you? We don't even like each other."

And the way she said the last sentence, curling her lips like the very thought repulsed her, made him even more determined to stick to his guns. He would bring her to heel if it killed him.

"Let's just say I've got my reasons." He spoke calmly, not giving away the fact that she'd just pissed him off. There would be time enough to get *his revenge for that transgression.*

"But I don't get it." As he walked back to his desk her eyes followed him, boring into him, never letting him go. He definitely had her attention now. "Ever since we met," she continued, "we've been at loggerheads. In fact, I wouldn't even be in your office right now if I weren't desperate."

Ridge smiled. "That, little Lani, is the operative word. The question is, how desperate are you?" He made sure to put emphasis on the word just so she didn't miss the point.

Lani's breathing was growing more and more agitated by the minute. Nostrils flaring, she got up and out of the chair and stood there, hands clenched at her sides. "You're sick. You know that?"

His smile deepened. "I may be," he said, his tone relaxed as ever, "but you're the one who's going to make this decision. Not me."

With a shrug he sank back into his chair and

looked at the seething woman standing in front of his desk. "My condition is on the table, Lani. Take it or leave it."

***

The chapter then ends like this:

While Chris and Minerva chattered away, Lani was busy opening the envelopes. So far so good. She was on envelope number three and all she'd seen were a newsletter, a credit card solicitation and a bank statement that was so depressing she barely spared it a glance. But envelope number four, that was the killer. It was from the company from which she'd leased the building and before she even opened it she knew what it would say inside.

Gritting her teeth, Lani went ahead and opened it anyway. "Pursuant to my letter dated February 15, this is to advise that your rent is now two months in arrears. If payment is not made within seven days of the date of this letter proceedings will be instigated to regain possession of the property and recover all outstanding amounts, including fees. In order to avoid this, please make arrangement to immediately make payment in full."

Despite herself, the hand that held the letter trembled. She'd expected a reprimand, definitely a warning, but not this. Seven days to find two months' rent plus fees? Where in heaven's name was she going to get that kind of money?

She knew she was at fault for paying the salaries – excluding hers – before taking care of the rent but Chris was a father with two young children. How could she tell him she wasn't going to pay him this month? And Minerva was working two jobs to put her little sister through college. How could she dash that dream?

Now, though, it seemed she would have to.

She'd gone without a salary for two months just to make ends meet but even that hadn't been enough. Without new funding the bank account had quickly run dry and even though she'd promised the leasing company she would catch up on the arrears within three months it was now obvious they weren't going to wait any longer. And who could blame them? When she'd made the promise, she'd been sure something would have come in. Now, over a dozen meetings later, nothing. Now she knew it had all been wishful thinking on her part.

"You okay, boss? You don't look so good." Minerva had turned toward her, a slight frown on her face.

For the second time that morning Lani found she had to explain herself to a member of her team. "I'm… fine, Minerva. Just some business I have to take care of."

And as she said the words, Lani's mind crept back to her meeting of the day before. Before he would give her any money, Ridge Kent wanted her to be his wife. But only for one year. She guessed she could manage...as long as they had a little talk first and she'd laid down the rules of this engagement. Under the circumstances, she could see no other way out of her dilemma.

And so, that conclusion reached, she made up her mind. She would do it. She would marry Ridge Kent. And, with all the wolves that were snarling at her door, the sooner the better.

So, we paid attention to the principal rule, the **Law of Firsts** – fascinate with your first sentence, your first paragraph, your first scene and your first chapter – making sure to use hooks along the way. Every element is an opportunity to further embed that hook.

You've now mastered **Judy Angelo's Law of Firsts**. Great job! Now it's time to dive into the story with the tantalizing storytelling techniques that make for a super-swift (not to mention, sweet) read.

CHAPTER FIVE

WRITING TECHNIQUES THAT TANTALIZE

We've already discussed the technique of hooking the reader with a promise of pleasure to come. Now, let's look at the technique of using **conflict** in your story. The majority of, if not all, romance readers are looking for a story in which the hero and heroine must work through their differences (established at the start of the story). The whole point of the story is to take us along their journey, to allow us insight into their growth along the way. That growth comes from overcoming problems and differences - in a word, conflict. ***Conflict is the spice*** that excites the reader and keeps her reading.

Create Conflict

Conflict may be in the form of situations, or in the form of emotional upheaval. It may be as basic as conflict between neighbors (e.g. **The Billionaire Next Door**). On the other hand, the conflict may be between rivaling corporations (**In Bed with the Enemy**). The conflict may arise when the tables are turned and the woman is now the one in charge; the man, traditionally in power, is now forced to abide by the rules of his new boss (**Bossing the Billionaire**). There are so many ways to create conflict. The key is to introduce a kind of conflict that you can sustain throughout the story. It can't just be a conflict where your characters will meet once, easily resolve the situation, and never meet again. It has to be conflict that must be worked out throughout the duration of the story. It must be maintained and sustained in order to keep your reader entertained.

Ideally, we also want a conflict situation where our characters are forced to be in close proximity to each other, whether for work, or in the place in which they reside, or in their activities. Trap them on a deserted island, if you must - but don't let them wander off into oblivion, simply because there is no need for them to be together. Keep creating conflict caused by their close proximity.

So, in a nutshell: ***Conflict is King***. Without it, you run the risk of having your story simply slide into the silence of oblivion.

Then, heighten the Conflict

And, now, we come to the all-important

close of the beginning section of your story. I know, I speak as if everything is important. And, yes, everything is.

It is the closing that provides the reader with the thrilling transition into the principal part of the story - the middle, the part where the bulk of the story is told, the part that so many writers love to hate. It is the infamous sagging middle.

But, before we get to said second stage, we have to first close the beginning section, and we need to do this on a high note. So, for the close of our beginning section (where the characters, the situation and the conflict are first introduced), we want to come up with the closing hook. Note well - the hook is not just for the start of our story. We hooked the reader at the start with our fantastic first sentence, our fascinating first scene, and our formidable first chapter. But our work is far from over. Along the way, with our creativity, we must keep our reader under our control, creating conflicts that continue to keep her enthralled, presenting promises of problems to appear along the path, masterfully mesmerizing her with maelstroms and mysteries.

Here are some examples of what I mean, from three of my stories:

First, in **Billionaire's Island Bride**, my heroine, who started out getting hurt by the hero and resenting him to the max, ends up becoming his wife - by blackmail. What this means is that, just as we are about to enter the middle of the story, both the writer and the reader have something new to look forward to. We're now entering the middle of the story, not with the same old conflict that was introduced at the start of the story. It's a whole new serious situation, a scenario that comes with a whole new set of conflicts that will maintain the reader's interest level at a consistent high.

And herein lies the **solution to the sagging middle** – keep the reader coming back for more, continuing to read because she craves the sweet satisfaction of a solution to the continued conflict. In short, she keeps reading because she just can't help it.

Here's an example from **Bossing the Billionaire**: the story starts with the man being his own boss, a billionaire boss, to boot. Shockingly, by the end of the first section, he is nothing more than a pawn in the heroine's power, working for her - at a menial job, at that. He is forced to wash dishes in a restaurant. Why is that? How will it end? So, in closing the first section with a new set of conflicts - and intrigue, to boot - the reader is forced to continue reading.

At the start of **Taming the Fury**, our woman is the one in charge - the boss, and a snarky one, at that. However, by the end of our first section, the tables are turned. To her horror, she finds herself working for the man! Now it's his turn to be boss. How is this going to end?

Conflicts – and then, there were more

You're off to a great start – creating conflict from the commencement of the story, then hooking and holding your reader by heightening the conflict. However, if you want to keep engaging your reader, you must keep adding new problems to the pile. Ramp up the troubles. Stir up the sorrows. That's your secret sauce.

The whole idea is to make matters worse for your characters, so much that they suffer. How else will you stir the sympathy of your reader? If your characters are all powerful and in total control at all times, then there's no reason to feel compassion or caring. Why do you think kids and teens these days are not so interested in Superman, but gravitate, instead, toward Iron Man and The Avengers? As my son told me, it's because Superman is too powerful. He can fly. He's super strong, super-fast, and he's got laser eyes. Who can defeat him? There's really no reason to feel sympathy or concern for a superhero who is invulnerable.

It's the same thing with your characters. If they do not experience trials and tribulations, suffering of some kind, then there's really no reason to feel either sympathy or empathy. So, add new miseries to the mix. Make life more difficult for them. Let the reader see how they grow and develop in the face of their struggles and challenges.

Insert Intrigue

On top of the troubles and trials that your characters face, it will be a plus to add a level of mystery or intrigue to your story. Troubles and challenges are great, but a mystery can heighten the interest even more. What if your character has a deep, dark, secret that could jeopardize his or her relationship?

What if there is another character who seems to have unexplained power over your hero or heroine? With these questions you are creating a conundrum, a cause for concern within the mind of the reader. It's a reason for your reader to care enough to want to finish the story.

Here's an example from **Billionaire's Island Bride**:

In this scene, the reader is made aware of a secret that is known only by the heroine and a woman who seems determined to put her relationship in jeopardy.

But Robin knew too much. And, if she felt that it would serve her purpose, she would be all too ready to spill those precious beans.

Erin had to take to think fast. How could she keep Robin from coming to the island?

After she hung up, Erin sat for a moment, deep in thought. This was not good. She did not like either one of her options. If she tried to keep Robin away, the girl would stir up trouble, for sure. And, if she came to the island and, even worse, came to stay at the house, Robin would find some way to make her life miserable. That was Robin.

Erin drew in a deep breath then stood up. She would talk to Dare and then she would start planning. She would have to keep Robin as busy as possible so she would have no opportunity to be alone with Dare. There was no telling what Robin would let slip. Erin could see it already. The coming week was going to be a nightmare.

With this passage, we are being introduced to a new level of intrigue, one that did not exist before, in this story. If the middle had had any inclination of beginning to sag, that is now warded off with the introduction of a new kind of mystery, one that would pique the curiosity of the reader, opening up a new and (intriguing) situation.

In **Taming the Fury**, the heroine's position of power crumbles right under her feet. She, who had always been the person in charge, the boss of a billion-dollar corporation, now finds herself in the hands of a man who used to be employed in an organization that she sponsors. She now has to report to him! And, after all she'd made him suffer in the past, she knows it's not going to be an easy experience.

With this major turning point, the reader has no opportunity to become bored. This reader, who had been reading about this powerful woman, now has his curiosity quickened. This is a new situation that takes him on a totally new journey.

This is what you need in the middle of your story, a situation that is bound to spark the curiosity of the reader, reel her in even farther, making it harder for her to slip away. Work it for all it's got. Under no circumstance should you lessen the tension. With this worsening situation, you've succeeded in sinking the hook even deeper, while giving yourself the opportunity to develop the story even more. Keep your story alive and well and even flourishing, with these major turning points.

Let's take a pause to distinguish between the turning point in your story and the turning point in the relationship. My example here focused on the turning point in the story, in relation to the action. It is the introduction of a new element into the story, something to wake it up, to make it fresh and vibrant again. It's a way to avoid the sagging middle. With the introduction of this brand-new element, the story is revitalized, so that the reader will receive a new jolt of joy and intrigue, and not be left to lag, thus losing interest. This turning point is what transpires in the story. It is where something unexpected happens, something that could prove quite significant.

The other type of turning point relates to the relationship between the hero and the heroine. With this turning point, the previous relationship, of course, one of conflict, may evolve into one free of discord; it may even be one of declared love.

However, that is not to say that the story is over. On the contrary, this is the point where you now present a new problem, one which may be in the form of the revival of the previous discord; it may be a previous problem in a new form; or it may be the creation of a totally new conflict or challenge.

In **Billionaire's Island Bride**, Erin and Dare must face the storm together – literally – when a dangerous hurricane hits the island. With this experience, having to rely on each other, they grow to trust each other, rely on each other, even love each other. Heaven. But then, just when the reader begins to relax, there is a new spin to the story, a cause for concern when a person from Erin's past shows up, threatening to mess up her marriage with the revelation of a seriously sensitive secret sure to sink her security with the love of her life.

More Techniques of which to Take Note

You would have already been using these in the first section of the story, but the middle is the place where you have ample opportunity to utilize your skills in writing, to showcase your writing style. This is where you put in practice the techniques you learned in school - pacing, character development, and the incorporation of setting into the story as a character in itself. It is the middle section of the story that needs these techniques the most. We must use every technique available to us, to avoid the sagging middle.

Pacing

Where pacing is concerned, I already indicated that the beginning of the story should, ideally, be at a rapid pace in order to capture and keep the interest of the reader. Start the story by stepping right into the middle of the action. Choose a significant scene to get started and, by that, I mean a point at which you can grab the attention of your reader. Pick a point where you can catch and keep her, by presenting either one of your principal players, whether the hero or the heroine, in a situation that's sure to spark curiosity. This is an essential element in getting her started on your story.

Then, of course, once she's stepped over the threshold, haul her inside and slam the door behind her with the fascinating first scene we spoke about. She may whirl around, seeking to escape to the household chores that await, but allow her no leeway. Let the creativity of your first chapter catch her mid-stride. Wrestle her to the ground with hints of intrigue, creative clues that capture her curiosity. From the start of the first chapter and right to the end, keep the action at a sprint by quickly creating a scene sizzling with tension, conflict and creative hooks.

By the middle of the story, the pace may slow somewhat. Now that you have the reader trapped, this is where you have the chance to turn the key in the lock by using the beauty of language to charm her even more. You can highlight the beauty of the setting. With the pacing slower, you now have the latitude to fully utilize your literary techniques such as alliteration, personification and simile. Even as you work to intrigue and charm your reader with your scintillating story, you can now use the middle section to impress her with your 'wicked' writing skills.

Which brings me to:

Alliteration

By now, you should have guessed that I'm a lover of alliteration (the repetition of the same sound in words in close proximity, in a sentence, scene or section of a story) – Hey, I did it again! Sorry, I can't help myself.

I acknowledge that each writer has his or her own style, so please don't take this as a hard and fast rule. I'm simply saying that we can seduce our reader with our story by using writing techniques that make the journey all the more pleasurable. It's up to each of us to find those techniques that work best for us, those techniques that fit our flow and writing style. For me, alliteration is a key component of my writing kit. I love the sound of words, the poetry present in prose. And, because I enjoy the rhythm of the right words at the right time, I feel that my reader will relate, and will relish my story even more, because of it.

Here's what I mean:

These are some samples, sections of sentences from a sweetly sensual scene in **To Tame a Tycoon**:

...then, slipping it into his mouth, he sucked softly and sweetly.

...his hands, the source of such sweetness that she....

And from **Daddy by December***:*

> *...caressing her, savoring her sweetness,,,*

What do you notice about these sensual scenes? Did you realize I was repeating the sound of the letter s? This was deliberate. In the same way that a sensual scene would involve seduction, softness and sweetness, I selected my words to support the seductive nature of the scene. In presenting my love scenes, where possible, I avoided hard sounds such as those created by words with the letters d, b and g, choosing, instead, to use the softer sound of the letter *s* as presented in words such as *soft*, *sweet*, *soothe* and *savour*, words so silky–smooth that they would seduce my reader into sliding into the sensuality of the scene.

In the same way that I use the soft s sound to support my sexy scenes, I use the hard and biting sounds of the letters b, g and d to support scenes characterized by conflict and rancor. You can hear it in such statements as,

a) *She bit down hard on her bottom lip*
b) *He grimaced and, with a guttural groan, he got up*

In these examples, the solid beat of the b sound and the grating of the g sound correspond very well with the mood of the message – nothing light and airy, but serious stuff.

To be honest, your reader may have no clue what you're doing, with all this alliteration. All she knows is that she loves the sound of the story. It's actually beautiful in her ears. It's just one additional element that will help make this a memorable experience for her.

Remember, she may be reading the story with her eyes but, as she reads, she's hearing her voice in her head. She's essentially reading aloud (albeit, in her mind). What this means is that we, as writers, must always bear in mind the importance of the sounds of our words.

Character Development

In the beginning section of the story, the reader would have been introduced to the hero and heroine. They may have been - in fact, they should have been - introduced with all their flaws. However, the middle of the story is where we see the character developing, growing from that feisty and even immature heroine to a woman who is stronger and wiser, able to make better decisions. Here is where the arrogant bachelor loses some of his hauteur and begins to flesh out as a more rounded character, one who your reader can really admire, one with whom she can fall in love.

Here is where you have the opportunity to show that the character who was initially so brash and uncontrollable, through his or her experience with the other key character, is growing more mature, more worthy of love. By the end of this section, the reader should be so in love with the character that he can't put the story down. He's forced to stay with the story because he must know what happens next.

In **Beauty and the Beastly Billionaire**, the cold and callous corporate head is taken down a notch when he encounters the audacious and defiant heroine who challenges his control and teaches him unexpected lessons in love. It is through the experience of being humbled by a woman, an experience so alien to him, that he makes that critical change that takes him along the path to progress. She, too, matures along the way, learning that defiance has its place. When it comes to controlling a dominant man, there's more than one way to skin the proverbial cat.

In **The Billionaire's Bold Bet** (my first foray into erotic romance), the brash billionaire must put aside petty play, rise to the occasion, and take control of the chaos he created. It is through his realization of the importance of honesty, and his admission of his own ills, that he is finally able to grow into a man worthy of the lady's love.

At the end of it all, the writer - the person steering the ship - must take the reader along a journey of change and growth, one where both hero and heroine develop past their previous problematic personalities and behaviors, and mature into well-rounded characters. It is the satisfying story of growth and change that makes the characters worthy of love.

Heighten the Intrigue

You've taken the reader thus far. You've caught her then corralled her. Here's where you place her in that pen from which there's no escape. A good mystery will do this.

In **Billionaires Island Bride**, Dare and Erin go through multiple harrowing experiences, including a hurricane. Of course, these shared experiences, as well as opportunities for intimacy, lead to a new level of connection between the two. This is where they begin to grow to trust each other. At this point, after all they have been through together, it seems that they will finally fall in love. They are bound to be together. As far as the reader can see, it is a done deal.

However, all is not rosy and peachy. That would be too easy. The reader needs to understand this. This is where you insert a new needle, one that punctures the smooth skin of this story that has just been going so well. This is where you insert a new mystery or reignite one that had fallen into the background. Bring it to the fore, making the reader wonder what the heck will come next. Rescue your story from the sagging middle by making a mystery work for you. Either that or make something go radically wrong.

Towards the end of **Billionaire's Island Bride**, a so-called friend of Erin turns up, the holder of a secret that Erin is sure will be the cause of disaster in her newfound relationship with Dare. Suddenly, the tension in the story is again heightened, sinking the hook back in. It's a new level of mystery, one that must be resolved. How can the reader leave you now?

This heightened intrigue is essential to the success of your story. In a word, it is the *antidote* to the poison of the sagging middle.

The Head-Turning Turning point

Turning points are super important to the middle of your novel. Remember, the challenge of this part of your story is that, if things continue along the same path, you will be in danger of allowing your reader to get so used to the story that they get, in a word, bored. You don't want to go there with them. No, you've reeled them in, you've taken them this far, and your goal is to take them all the way to the end, kicking and screaming but coming along, nonetheless.

By the middle of the story, make something significant happen. Remember the example of **Taming the Fury.** In the middle of the mayhem created by the crabby heroine, the tables are turned when the story swerves to a surprising situation, one where her position of power crumbles right under her feet. She, who had always been the person in charge, the captain of a billion-dollar corporation, now finds herself in the hands of a man who used to be employed by an organization that she sponsors. With this major turning point, the reader has no opportunity to become bored. She, who had been reading about this powerful woman, must now adjust. She now has her curiosity piqued. This is a new situation that takes her on a totally new journey.

This is what you need in the middle of your story, a situation that is bound to spark the curiosity of the reader, reeling her in even further, making it harder for her to slip away. Work it for all it's got. Under no circumstance should you should you lessen the tension. You've now sunk the hook deeper, while giving yourself the opportunity to develop the story even more, keeping your story alive and well and even flourishing.

This is the power of the properly positioned turning point.

The Black Moment

Now that you've taken the reader on a journey from which there is no turning back, this is the moment for…wait for it… the black moment This is the point where, after making Reader Dearest so comfortable that she's now relaxing, thinking all is well and the hero and heroine will live happily ever after, you burst her bubble.

Hand in hand, strolling off into the sunset? No such thing. That would be too easy. Now is the time when you throw things upside down and make the reader gasp in shock. Here's where there's that deep dive into distress. Now's the time when you throw something into the mix, something that makes it seem like there will be no hope for their future.

This is the point where you make the reader say, what the heck? How will they get out of this mess? It may distress your reader but it's for a good reason. It will keep the interest level so high that *Dear Reader* will be forced to carry on. There's no way that she'll put this book down. Not at this point.

Here's an illustration of what I mean…

In **Naughty by Nature,** after Tessa and Wolf get to what one would think is the point of no return, when Wolf finally decides to give up his 'wild' ways and give in to the wiles of his wicked little temptress, he is blindsided when our goodly heroine throws an unexpected monkey wrench into the mix, introducing a situation that suddenly seems hopeless. Immediately, the reader's complacency is converted into tension, a tight rope that's tied around her ankle, that takes her to the very end.

What does the twist of the black moment do? It makes the reader root for the hero and heroine, and their love. Against all odds, the reader now wants these two beloved characters to be rewarded with the love that they deserve. If the reader had been upset with either one, or both of them, not now. Now she wants them to be together. For good. They've been through too much.

Call this our pièce de résistance, that one thing that will make the reader totally invested in the story. So, make it good. Make that twist toward the

end of the story so painful, and make it so unlikely that they will overcome, that the reader will have to continue reading in order to
find out how this will end. This is the climax of your story, the high point after which your reader will be rewarded with a satisfying resolution.

.

CHAPTER SIX

THE END

The Roller Coaster Ride

Imagine a roller coaster. In the same way that a roller coaster takes us up to a certain height and then drops us down, the story must do the same. It must take the reader to a certain level of tension and then release her - just a little bit. How do you do release her? You resolve a minor issue.

But then, as soon as she's gotten used to that relaxed atmosphere, that respite, she's off on another hike - up an even steeper incline, one that leaves her heart pounding; it is a tension which is even tighter than the one before. You do this by creating a new tension, a new problem that will perturb. A bigger problem.

Then, this tension is relaxed when the problem is resolved; the reader is released. This time, she's allowed to fall even farther down the hill. Then, as soon as she begins to get used to being at the bottom of the valley, she is made to climb again, now up an even steeper incline, one that she wonders if she will survive. What have you done to her? You've presented an even bigger problem that she must now ponder.

The next drop is swift and scary. And, so, goes the story, with a tension that terrifies, even as it titillates. But it's this sudden swoop down that captivates and enthralls her, that makes her know that there's no way she can let go. Not now. By the time the novel is brought to its rewarding resolution, the reader can't even make a move to get up and get going. She's got to sit there, for a moment, letting it all sink in, letting the waves of wonder wash over her.

From the series, **Billionaire Bachelorettes of Bel-Air**, the story, **In Bed with the Enemy**, takes the reader on a roller coaster ride that has the hero in constant conflict with the heroine. The story continues to develop until he finds he is falling head over heels in love. But then he falls again, and this time he is reeling and bruised from a betrayal so brutal that it seems there is no hope.

In short, the roller coaster ride, all that tension interspersed with moments of respite, will offer the reader just enough ease to catch her breath as she reads your fast-paced story. The key, though, is to keep her gripping the bar as the roller coaster ride rapidly picks up pace, hurtling her forward, never allowing her the opportunity to abandon the story.

With continued conflicts (whether situational or emotional), strategically placed hooks and incidents of intrigue, the roller coaster ride will be both thrilling and rewarding.

The Critical Close

Now, we've come to the critical portion of the story. All right, all right, I know. I speak as if each part of the story - the beginning, the middle, and the end - are important. They are. They all are. And, so, regardless of a super-strong start and a formidable middle, we've got to make sure that the conclusion is equally strong, even more so.

We'll start with a strong close to our character development.

By the time we get to this part of the story, the characters should have grown to the point where the reader is able to recognize that this is a new person, one who has matured with all that he has gone through, with the relationship that should, by now, have faced formidable challenges.

Maybe those challenges are still hanging

in the air. Maybe they're still quite alive. But, by this time, the reader would have realized that the characters are quite different from those with whom she began the journey. It is in this section that all mysteries that are still open must be resolved. Not too early, though. The main mystery, the main issue, should be held out until as close to the end as possible. The last thing you want is for the reader to feel that he can go before the story has ended. That is why it is critical that the mystery be maintained as close to the end as possible, in order to ensure that the reader remains in the camp and never strays.

By this time, all minor matters should have been resolved, leaving only the major one as the focus of the story, so that the reader will not be distracted by the mundane. Here's an example:

In **Billionaire's Island Bride**, along the way there are hints about a deep, dark secret that can jeopardize the happiness of the heroine and hero, Erin and Dare. However, it is not until the final chapters of the story that we get the details of the dilemma that Erin has been trying so hard to delay, the secret she's been trying to suppress. If the reader had thought the story was over, with the re-introduction of this mystery, she gets a rude awakening. She now knows that, if she is going to rest easy tonight, she must have an answer before she closes the covers.

With the unsolved mystery re-opened at the end of this story, do you see what I mean about sustaining the suspense by leaving the main mystery unsolved until the closing section? It's not until the very end, when the reader can do no more than hang in there, that I really bring the mystery to a resolution and the story to a close.

The Rewarding Resolution

Here is where we bring the story to a satisfying end. Of course, this is where the hero and heroine commit to each other. This is the point at which we know there is no turning back; they will be together, there is no longer any doubt about that.

Here's the satisfying resolution to **Tamed by the Billionaire**:

Serena woke to the most beautiful day of spring she'd ever seen. It was also the happiest day of her life. Today she would marry the man who had captured her mind, her heart and soul.

She hopped out of bed and ran over to the window to breathe in the fragrance of the flowers under her window. Simply delicious.

Serena smiled as she stared out her bedroom window. She'd moved back home to spend time with her father before the wedding but last night was the last she'd spend under this roof as Serena Van Buren. By the end of the day she would be Serena Steele.

She leaned out of the window to get a better view of the south lawn. The decorators were already bustling about, making sure the trellis and its trimmings were in order. It would be a garden wedding right on the lawn where she used to play with her mother. Maybe her mother would look down on her today and send her wedding blessings on the breeze.

There was a knock at her door and Serena spun around to see her father peeping in. "Ready for your big day, Princess?"

"Oh, Daddy, it's like I've been ready all my life." She went to him and stepped into his arms. When he released her from the hug she saw that his eyes were shiny with unshed tears.

"Your mother would be so happy," he said, looking down at her with a smile. "You made an excellent choice for a husband."

Serena's eyes widened. "I did? You sure you're not upset?"

"Upset?" Richard laughed. "I couldn't have made a better choice myself. In fact, there's something I must tell you." His eyes sparkled with mischief. "I was hoping for this outcome all along. I knew if there was one man who could bring the woman out of my little girl, it was Roman Steele."

"Daddy, did you set me up?" Serena pouted but a smile tickled her lips, making her mirth obvious.

"No, but I'd like to think your mother had a hand in this. Today more than ever I feel her presence and I think she's smiling."

Serena smiled up at her father and now it was her turn to blink back happy tears. "I feel her, too, Daddy. And I know today in the *garden she'll be right there with me as I take my big step."*

Then, as the birds whistled in the tree outside her window, Serena turned and looked out at the sun rising in the brilliant blue sky. "Thanks, Mom," she whispered, "for finding me the best man I could ever want."

This is where you can also provide a peek into the future, into what lies ahead for these key characters who we've grown to love. In looking into the future, you bring the story to an even more satisfying close.

Here's an example, from **Bedding her Billionaire Boss**:

"Mommy, Daddy's being bad again."

Dana sighed as the kitchen door burst open and six-year-old Maya and her four-

year-old brother dashed in.

"Yeah," Michael said, "he's hugging the ball."

"Hogging the ball," Maya corrected, rolling her eyes. Then she put her hands on her hips and set her mouth in her classic pout. "Mama," she whined, dragging the word out so far it was like fingernails on a chalkboard, "make him stop."

Dana pursed her lips then stuck her head out the window. "Daddy," she called out, her voice stern, "behave."

"Aw, spoilsport." Rock yelled back from the bottom of the garden. "You're taking sides with them. No fair."

"Don't let Mommy come out there," she yelled back. "It won't be pretty."

At her words, Rock came bounding up the garden, a huge grin on his face. "Okay, guys," he said, "it's all yours." He threw the beach ball up into the air and let it fall back down to the ground.

"Yay." With whoops of joy, the children scampered out to scoop up the coveted toy.

As soon as they were out the door, Rock sauntered in, walked up to Dana as she tore up leaves of lettuce, and hugged her from behind.

"What you gonna do?" he whispered. "Lock me up?"

She gave a snort. "I've done it before."

For that, he bent his head and gave her a nip on the neck. "So, let's go play lock-up. I've got handcuffs."

Dana opened her eyes wide and dropped her handful of lettuce back into the bowl. Then she turned to give her husband a stern look. Or, at least, she tried. It was kind of hard to be stern when you had a grin on your face. "Rock, behave. The children-"

"Are gone back down to the bottom of the garden. They'll be busy with that ball for a while. And besides, Nanny's with them." He pulled her into his arms. "What say we run upstairs? You can punish me for being a bad boy. Without the police this time."

That made Dana laugh out loud.

"Naughty, naughty."

Rock didn't wait to hear any more. He swept her up into his arms and took the stairs two at a time. And, as he took her into the room and laid her on the bed, Dana thanked the stars for her wonderful family and this man whose love was hot and passionate and absolutely crazy.

Rock St. Stephens, the love of her life, would never escape her...even if it meant keeping him under lock and key.

He was hers – to have and to hold and to love – forever.

By the time your story ends, your reader should be totally satisfied, not feeling cheated in any way...

...which brings me to the question of mysteries. The last thing you want to do is to set up a mystery, not answer it, and leave the reader hanging at the end of the journey. The only way I would recommend that strategy is if you have the sequel ready and waiting, so that the reader can devour it immediately thereafter. Otherwise, you risk losing that reader. Avoid dissatisfaction at all costs. Seek to satisfy your reader with a sensational story that has an excellent ending, one that leaves nothing to speculation.

Are you with me so far? Do you understand my direction? Go ahead. Give it a try. Finish that story and put it to the test. Put it out there - with its hooks, conflicts and intrigue. See what a difference these techniques make, in getting your readers on board, and then committed to crossing the finish line with you.

She wants the characters to end up together. Trust me on that. And, if you give her all the key elements that will keep her rooting for them, she will never bail out of your boat.

Now let's get started on writing that riveting story!

CHAPTER SEVEN

KEY LEARNINGS

Key Learnings/ Critical Elements

So, what are the critical elements we've discussed?

Commence with Clarity

- **A creative opening** to capture the attention – commencing with conflict creates a great opening. It captures the attention.

- **Clear goals** for each of your main characters is a great place to start. Opposing goals? Even better! This keeps the conflict constantly going, getting the reader all hot and bothered. Cool!
- **Creation of captivating characters,** of whom you can't get enough.

Connect Creatively (Using Hooks)

– A **first sentence** that grabs the attention and makes the reader want to read on.

- A **first paragraph** that heightens the intrigue so that the reader will not want to turn back.
- A **first scene** that sets the stage for a sizzling story.
- A **first chapter** that establishes the fact that this story is so full of fire

and intrigue that the reader will not even think of abandoning the boat at this point.

- **Closing hooks** (questions) at the end of each scene and each chapter, the technique that guarantees the return of the reader (if she ever left at all).

Capitalize on Calls to Continue (reading)

- **A captivating middle** in which the tension tightens constantly, never lagging.
- **Continued conflicts** that keep the reader reading. Never allow her level of interest to wane.
- **Close proximity for your key characters** – set up situations where they must always be in each

other's presence. Therein lies one of the keys to conflict – they constantly run into each other, always rubbing each other the wrong way. Never give them the chance to avoid each other.

- **Clever conversation** – make sure the dialogue is dynamic, allowing your characters to demonstrate their personalities, their concerns and also their back stories (history and heritage – show the reasons why they are the way they are).

- **Clear character development** – show how your characters grow and change with their various experiences (and we are, of course, expecting them to change for the better, with time and trials and testing).

- **Clear clues along the way,** when you've introduced intrigue into your story.

- **Contrasts** – of personality, of experiences, of points of view. Use these to clearly demonstrate the cause for the conflicts that keep cropping up.
- **Concerns** – don't make life too easy for your characters. Keep your story spicy with plenty of problems along the way. A tear-jerker moment can also work well to solicit the sympathy of your reader, make her connect with the character who is suffering.

Create a Compelling Close

- **A Close that includes a reversal,** a situation that seems to unravel all the progress that has been made – a distressing (and frustrating) black moment – one that will make the final resolution all the more satisfying and sweet.

- A **Close that is concrete**, complete, clarifying and satisfying, leaving no question unanswered, no mystery unsolved, no issue unresolved.

- **Clear indication that the couple will finally enjoy an HEA** (a happily ever after ending).

.

CHAPTER EIGHT

WRAP UP

Okay, so you stuck with me through thick and thin, right to the very end. Good. Now you know how to hook your reader and have her take that thrilling ride with you.

With all these hooks, some subtle and some not so subtle, *Dear Reader* is now fully engaged, staying with your story from start to finish.

But, hold on. This guide is not yet over. There's just one last hook I want to throw out there - the hook that will get your reader to go searching for the next story in your series.

The 'Get the Next Story' Hook:

Here are some suggestions:

- Consider writing your story with a secondary character strong enough to merit a story of his/her own. This will provide a springboard from which you can launch another story, a whole new story, maybe even a series (e.g. Tessa of **Naughty by Nature,** who was a friend from **To Catch a Man - in Thirty Days or Less)**. Suggested characters from whom to spin off – best friends, siblings, co-workers. Make that character so intriguing that the reader will be eager to learn more about him/her.
- Regardless of whether the next story features a follow-up character, as

soon as your second story is in stores, go back and insert the link in the back of the previous book. Your reader will want more reading material. Let her not have to leave your camp to get it.

Now get going with your next thrilling masterpiece! Congratulations on taking your next step along your writing journey.

I look forward to seeing your sizzling story in stores!

Would you like to keep in touch? I would love
to hear from you!

You may reach me at

judyangeloauthor@gmail.com

or get writing tips and book updates at

www.judyangelo.blogspot.com

e